POEMS ABOUT ANIMALS

WAYLAND

www.waylandbooks.co.uk

First published in Great Britain in 2015 by Wayland
Copyright © Wayland, 2015

Editor: Victoria Brooker
Designer: Lisa Peacock

ISBN: 978 0 7502 9178 1
Library eBook ISBN: 978 0 7502 9179 8

10 9 8 7 6 5 4 3 2 1

Wayland, an imprint of Hachette Children's Group
Part of Hodder & Stoughton
Carmelite House
50 Victoria Embankment
London EC4Y 0DZ

An Hachette UK Company
www.hachette.co.uk
www.hachettechildrens.co.uk

Printed and bound in China

Acknowledgements:
The Compiler and Publisher would like to thank the authors for allowing their poems to appear in
this anthology. Poems © the authors. While every attempt has been made to gain permissions and
provide an up-to-date biography, in some cases this has not been possible and we apologise for
any omissions. Should there be any inadvertent omission, please apply to the Publisher for rectification.
'The Terrible Ten!' by James Carter taken from 'I'm A Little Alien!' by James Carter (Janetta Barry Books/Frances
Lincoln) copyright@2014; 'Komodo Dragon' first appeared in Wild! Rhymes That Roar, chosen by James Carter and
Graham Denton, Macmillan Children's Books, 2009; 'A Bear in his Underwear' by Brian Moses, taken from 'The
Monster Sale' (Frances Lincoln) 2013; 'How to Spot a Kangaroo' from 'Snail Stampede and Other Poems' by Robert
Scotellaro (Hands Up Books, 2004).

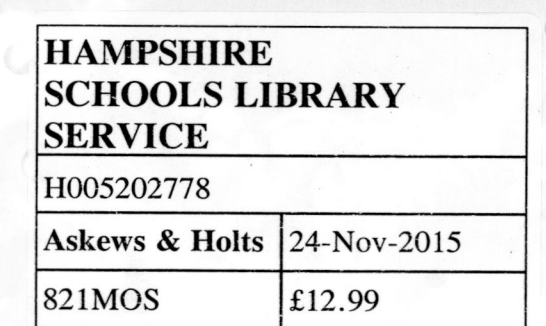

Contents

The Terrible Ten!

One!
Do a *stroll* like a tiger

Five!
Do a *stretch* like a lion

Two!
Do a *grrr* like a bear

Four!
Do a *leap* like a hare

Three!
Do a *scuttle* like a spider

Six!

Do a *flap* like a bat

Ten!

Do a *waddle* like a hen

Seven!

Do a *swoop* like a barn owl

Nine!

Do a *sway* like an eagle

Eight!

Do a *nibble* like a rat

Then it might be nice
just once or twice
to do the ten again!

James Carter

On My Way from School

On my way from school I saw a cat
It was a fat cat
It was a black, fat cat
It was a big, black, fat cat
It was a hairy, big, black, fat cat
It was a scary, hairy, big, black, fat cat
It was a mean, scary, hairy, big, black, fat cat
It was *my* mean, scary, hairy, big, black, fat cat
    called Cuddles
And she followed me home.

Roger Stevens

Animal Riddles

It has four hooves, a tail of course.
Who wants to ride this lovely...

It's dressed in feathers, rhymes with carrot
sharp curved beak, must be a...

It's long, and skinny as a rake.
Don't let it bite, must be a...

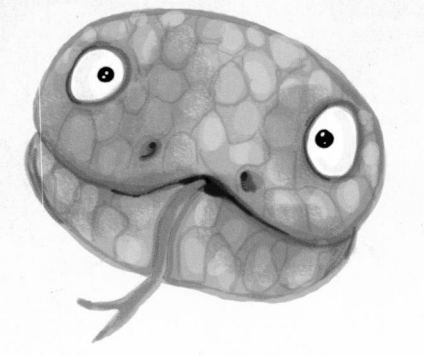

It's small and scuttles round the house.
A long, thin tail, must be a...

Long ears, bright eyes, a hopping habit,
round white tail, must be a...

You count them when you're trying to sleep.
Those woolly jumpers, must be...

Marian Swinger

9

My Dog

My dog is cuter
then a baby snuggling with a teddy bear.

My dog is naughtier
than a boy putting a rat in his teacher's handbag.

My dog is fluffier
than a bed made out of cotton wool.

My dog is braver
than a medieval knight riding into battle.

My dog is sillier
than a clown doing a backflip with his pants down.

My dog eats more
than a Tyrannosaurus at a buffet.

My dog barks louder
than the eruption of twenty volcanoes.

But enough about that —
you should see my cat!

Joshua Seigal

11

Sad Rabbit

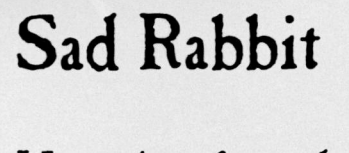

How they fussed over me
When I was new:
Filled up my bowl –
Played with me too;
Fed me green leaves,
Dandelions and such,
Stroked my long ears,
Cleaned out my hutch.
Life was great then
But gradually
They found other things
And lost interest in me.
They had new bikes, a football,
A computer to use –
A sad, lonely rabbit
Was yesterday's news.
Now they don't even
Bother to come.

Who brings my food?
Not them, but their Mum.
She says, "It's *your* rabbit,
It's really not fair.
It needs a new home
And someone to care."
So perhaps I'll be moving
To someone quite new
Who'll care for a rabbit —
What about you?

Eric Finney

A Bear in his Underwear

You shouldn't point and you mustn't stare
if you see a bear in his underwear.

It's really rude to take a peep
at a bear just woken from winter sleep.

A bear who's out to test the air
while wondering what clothes to wear.

For him it will be a big surprise,
he'll be trying to rub the sleep from his eyes.

He'll be thinking of honey and hoping to find
something sweet that the bees left behind.

So don't be surprised if when you wave
he disappears into his cave.

He'll really be in no mood to talk
till he's properly dressed and off for a walk.

So if you see a bear with holes in his vest
and pants a long way past their best.

Pass him by, just leave him there,
if you see a bear who's almost bare!

Brian Moses

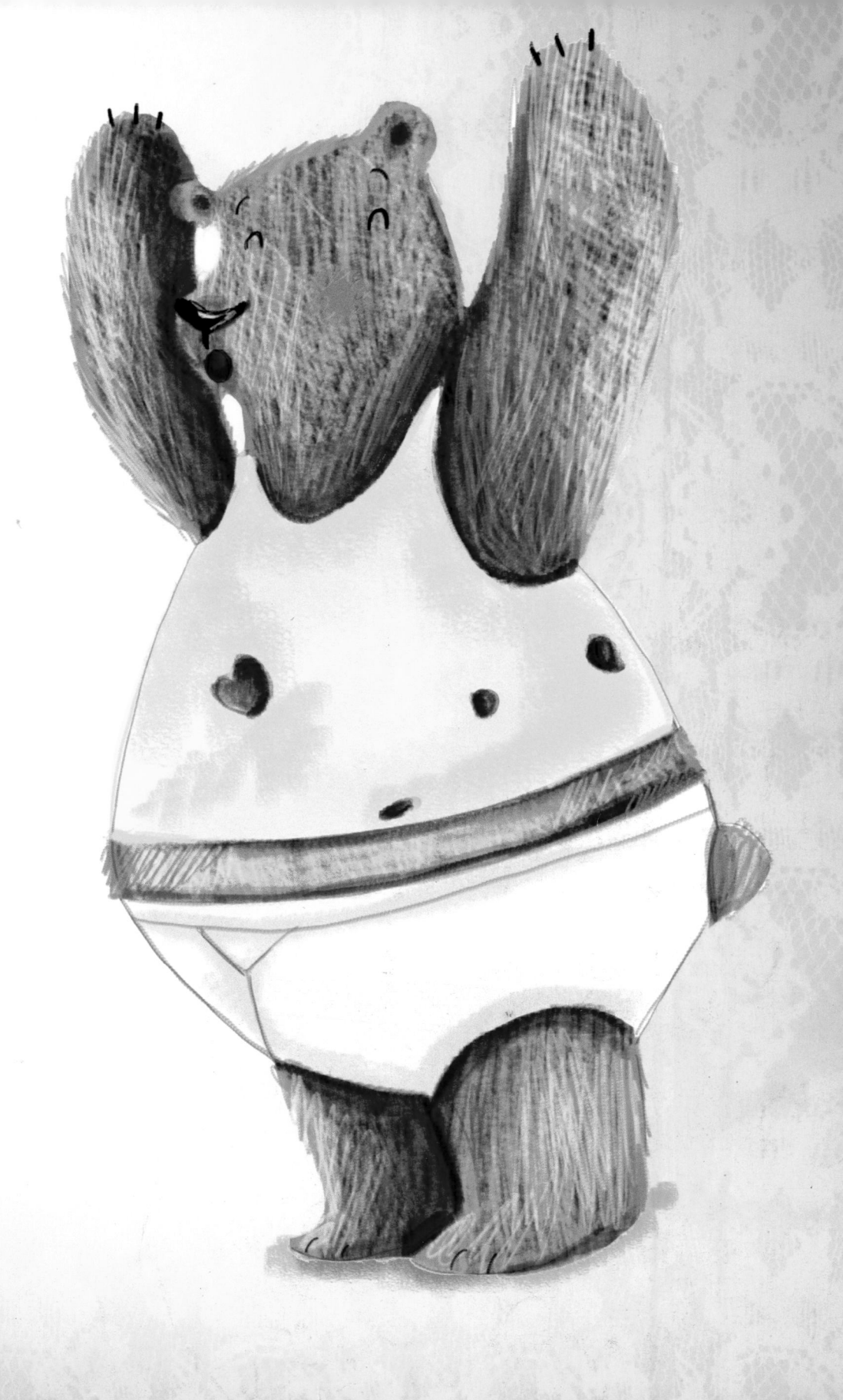

Komodo Dragon

Here be creatures
    ten feet long
Here be beasts
    immense and strong
Here be huge and
    brawny tails
Here be skin
    with brownish scales

Here be brutes
    who overpower
Here be monsters
    that devour
Here be jaws
    with lethal bites
Here be giant
    appetites

Here be kings
  from days of old
Here be tales
  the ancients told
Here be teeth
  of dinosaurs
Here be feet
  with razor claws

Here be foul
  and fetid breath
Here be eyes
  as cold as death
Here be legends
  newly born
Here be dragons
  you've been warned!

Graham Denton

I'm A Giraffe

I'm a giraffe,
with my head in the sky;
watch me stretch my neck up high.

I'm a kangaroo,
with my legs so strong:
watch me as I bounce along.

I'm a chimpanzee,
with my hands down low;
swinging my arms wherever I go.

I'm a snake,
with my body on the ground:
watch me as I slither around.

I'm a rabbit,
with my ears that flop;
everybody knows how to bunny hop.

I'm a crocodile,
with my jaws open wide;
why don't you come and look inside?

Mike Jubb

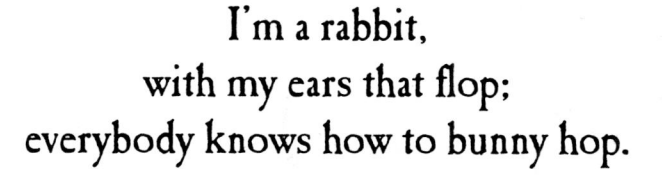

Hungry Crocodile

Float, float, float, hidden by the boat,
Is the hungry crocodile,
Scales, scales, scales, from the nose to the tail
Of the hungry crocodile,
Stare, stare, stare, goes the scary glare
Of the hungry crocodile,
Smack, smack, smack, goes the crinkly back
Of the hungry crocodile.
Scratch, scratch, scratch, goes the long claw catch
Of the hungry crocodile.
Snap, snap, snap, goes the sharp tooth trap
Of the hungry crocodile
SNAP!

Actions, the children: -
Line 1: Pretend to float, fingers 'rippling' under chins.
Line 3: Point to their noses then feet
Line 5: Stare with menace!
Line 7: Wriggle their backs/bottoms
Line 9: Pretend to scratch with curled fingers
Line 11: With outstretched arms, they bring their hands together on each snap like jaws
Line 13: As above for one last, almighty SNAP!

Coral Rumble

If You Should Meet a Crocodile

If you should meet a crocodile
Don't take a stick and poke him
Ignore the welcome in his smile
Be careful not to stroke him
For as he sleeps upon the Nile
He thinner gets and thinner
So whenever you meet a crocodile
He's ready for his dinner!

Anon

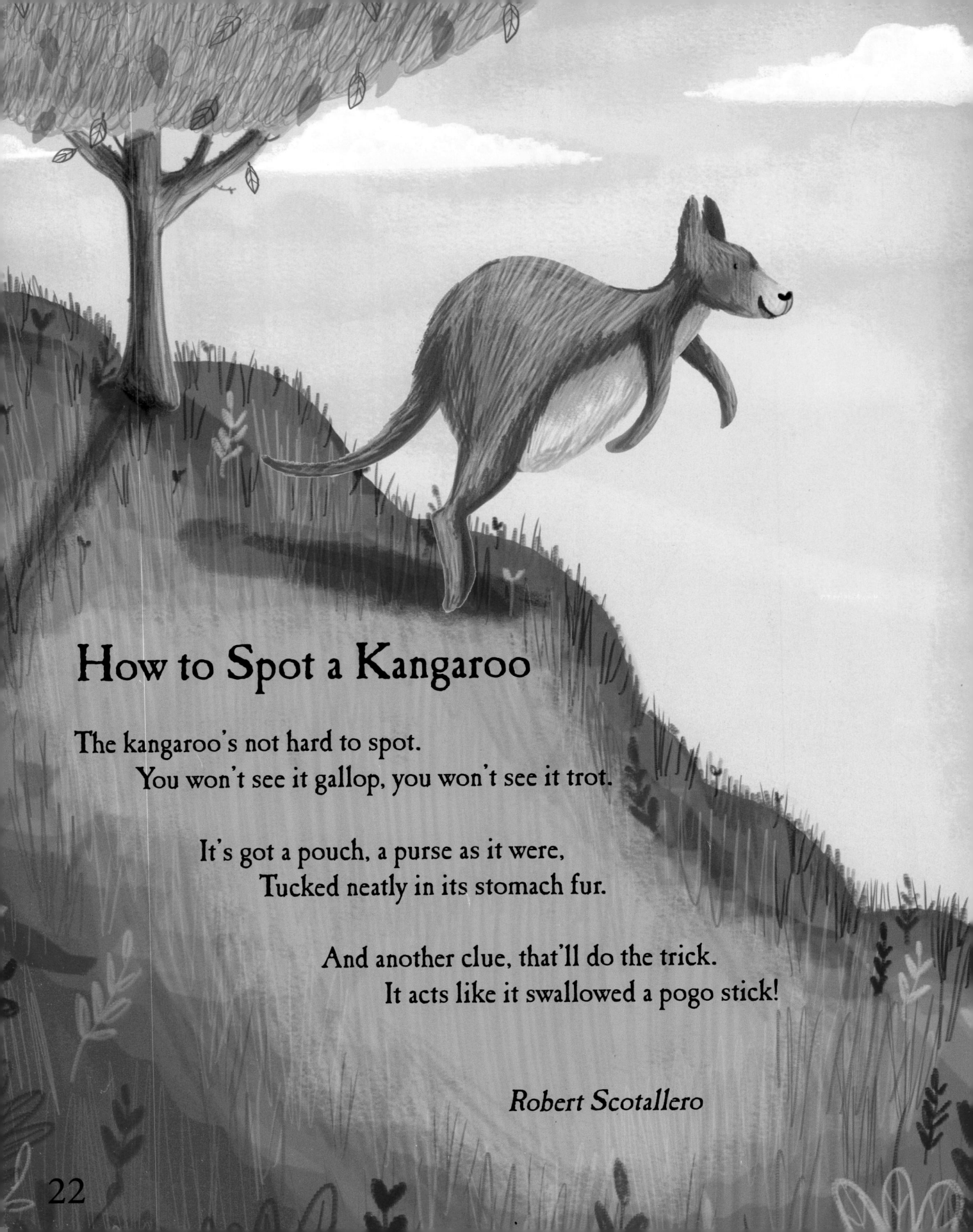

How to Spot a Kangaroo

The kangaroo's not hard to spot.
    You won't see it gallop, you won't see it trot.

    It's got a pouch, a purse as it were,
        Tucked neatly in its stomach fur.

        And another clue, that'll do the trick.
          It acts like it swallowed a pogo stick!

                Robert Scotallero

Caterpillar

Brown and furry
    Caterpillar in a hurry,
Take your walk
    To the shady leaf, or stalk,
Or what not,
    Which may be the chosen spot.
No toad spy you,
    Hovering bird of prey pass by you;
Spin and die,
    To live again a butterfly.

Christina Rossetti

Swish Swash!

Up before the wallabies,
up before the gnus.
In and out and all about
through the caribous.

Polishing an elephant,
flossing a giraffe,
tick-a-ling hyenas
just to get a laugh.

Swishing and swashing,
underneath the minks.
Swishing and swashing,
'Morning, Mister Lynx.'

Dabbing spot remover
on a leopard's tail,
vacuuming the feathers
of a nightingale.

Buffing up the pandas,
laundering the bats,
stop to a pat a platypus,
scale the mountain cats.

Swishing and swashing,
under the impala.
Swishing and swashing,
'Pardon me, Koala.'

Brush a little harder —
got to get it right -
can't have a crocodile
whose teeth aren't white.

Tidy up the antelope,
manicure the bear,
spring-clean the ceiling
of the old wolf's lair.

With a swish and a swash,
and a golly, golly gosh —
what a great day
for an animal wash!

Bill Condon

Tiger

A tiger is hiding there, under my bed,
with a black and gold body and huge stripy head;
and when it grows dark he gets bolder, it seems,
for he climbs on my quilt and slides into my dreams.

The tiger's decided he's coming downstairs,
but his sharp claws will scratch all the tables and chairs,
and he'll go in the kitchen and eat all the cakes —
that's after he's finished the chicken and steaks.

When he's eaten, the tiger goes running outdoors
and he rolls on the grass and he stretches his claws,
and his purr is as loud as an engine, his eyes
are brighter than stars in the blackest of skies.

I talk to the tiger each time he appears
and I stroke his great head and I fondle his ears;
and my tiger's as massive as massive can be.
So why is it nobody sees him but me?

Alison Chisholm

Animal Farewells

In a while, crocodile
See you later, small pond skater
Keep it real, you cool seal
Gotta go, my chum rhino
All my love, my sweet friend dove
Happy trails, little snails
Hey, hang loose, my darling goose
Well, see you then, you happy hen
Chin chin, penguin

My best wishes, titchy fishes
Goodbye for now, big brown cow
Love your pyjamas, you funky llamas
Time to set sail, you graceful whale
See you soon, sweet racoon
Love and hugs, little slugs
See you there, my lovely bear
Love you lots, ocelots
Time for sleep, my little sheep xxx

Kate Snow

Further information

Once a poem in this book has been read, either individually, in groups, or by the teacher, check with the children that they have understood what the poem is about. Ask them to point out any difficult lines or words and explain these. Ask the children how they feel about the poem. Do they like it? Is there a certain section or line of the poem that they particularly enjoy?

James Carter's 'The Terrible Ten' is an action rhyme that children will enjoy performing. A similar poem could be compiled from children's ideas about how other creatures move or sound. 'On My Way from School' by Roger Stevens is also a good model to inspire children's own poems.

> On my way from school I saw a gorilla,
> It was a scary gorilla,
> It was a hairy, scary gorilla,
> It was a huge, hairy, scary gorilla,
> It was a …

Children will enjoy solving the riddles in Marian Swinger's 'Animal Riddles' and again may like to make up more of their own. Talk about rhyme and how these riddles have a lovely rhythm, then write one with the children:

> It sleeps in the sun, or lies on the mat,
> Furry and purry, it must be a …

Show children that Joshua Seigal's 'My Dog' isn't a rhyming poem until it gets to the last two lines. However, once read out they should spot that it has a rhythm. Can anyone spot that it is the repetition of 'My dog is….' that gives it its rhythm? Children can write about their own pets in a similar way.

'Sad Rabbit' by Eric Finney is an excellent poem for discussion. Is it fair to keep a pet if you lose interest in it? Should you let someone else care for something that's yours? What might be best for the rabbit in this poem?

'A Bear in His Underwear' by Brian Moses is written in rhyming couplets. Ask children to pick out the rhyming words. Could they change the rhymes?

> You shouldn't point and you mustn't look
> if you see a bear reading a book.

'Komodo Dragon' by Graham Denton works well as a read aloud for two voices. One voice would say the 'Here be…' line with a second voice for the rest of the line. Mike Jubb's poem 'I'm a Giraffe' is also the sort of poem that can be a model for children's own poetry.

Coral Rumble's 'Hungry Crocodile' is an action poem. Children could learn this poem off by heart. They could also learn 'How to Spot a Kangaroo' by American poet Robert Scotallero, perhaps jumping up and down on the last line when they recite it!

'Caterpillar' by Christina Rossetti is the oldest poem in the book. Encourage children to find out about her. 'Swish Swash!' by Australian poet Bill Condon is simply great fun and would make a great wall display combined with children's own illustrations.

Read the classic picture book 'The Tiger Who Came for Tea' by Judith Kerr alongside 'Tiger' by Alison Chisholm. 'Animal Farewells' by Kate Snow could lead to children discovering other ways to say farewell to different creatures – All for now, spotted cow/ cheerio, big black crow.

Encourage children to look for further examples of poems about animals. These can be copied out and then illustrated. Build up a collection of poems and let children talk about their favourites. Let them practise reading and performing the poems adding actions and percussion accompaniment if appropriate.

About the Poets:

James Carter is the liveliest children's poet and guitarist in town. He's travelled nearly everywhere from Loch Ness to Southern Spain with his guitar, Keith, to give performances and workshops in schools and libraries and also festivals. An award-winning poet, his titles are published by Frances Lincoln, Macmillan and Bloomsbury. Find him, read him, hear him at: www.jamescarterpoet.co.uk

Alison Chisholm gets inspiration for her poems from her twin cats, Byron and Shelley. When she isn't writing poetry, she's usually to be found reading it or talking about it. Recently retired, she's still trying to decide what to do when she grows up, but as long as it includes poetry she'll be happy.

Bill Condon and his wife, the well known children's author, Dianne (Di) Bates, live on the south coast of New South Wales, Australia. They are both full-time writers. Bill's work includes novels, short stories, and collections of plays and poetry. He was the winner of the Prime Minister's Literary Award in 2010 for young adult fiction. His latest book, *The Simple Things*, was shortlisted for Australia's Children's Book Council Awards in 2015.
www.enterprisingwords.com.au

Graham Denton is a writer and anthologist of poetry for children, whose poems feature in numerous publications both in the UK and abroad. As an anthologist, his compilations include *Orange Silver Sausage: A Collection of Poems Without Rhymes* (Walker Books), *My Cat is in Love with The Goldfish* (A & C Black) and *When Granny Won Olympic Gold* (A&C Black). Most recently, Graham celebrated the release of the first full collection of his own funny verses, *My Rhino Plays The Xylophone,* published by A&C Black. He has also twice been short listed for the UK's CLPE Poetry Award.

Eric Finney wrote a number of books for children including *Billy and Me at the Church Hall Sale* and *Billy and Me and the Igloo.* His poems can be found in many anthologies. He was fond of walking and nearly always returned from his walks with ideas for poems. He lived in Ludlow.

Mike Jubb's poems are widely anthologised and he has a picture book, *Splosh,* published by Scholastic.

Brian Moses lives in Burwash in Sussex where the famous writer Rudyard Kipling once lived. He travels the country performing his poetry and percussion show in schools, libraries and theatres. He has published more than 200 books including the series of picture books *Dinosaurs Have Feelings Too* (Wayland). His favourite animal is his fox red labrador, Honey. www.brianmoses.co.uk

Christina Rossetti (1830-94) was an English poet who published a number of books and rhymes for young children including *Sing Song* and *Goblin Market* - a fairy story in verse.

Coral Rumble has had three collections of children's poetry published, and is featured in numerous anthologies. She often writes for CBeebies TV and Radio. In 2014, Coral's first picture book, *The Adventures of the Owl and the Pussycat,* written in partnership with her illustrator daughter, was long-listed for Oscar's First Book Prize. Michael Rosen has said, 'Rumble has a dash and delight about her work'.

Robert Scotellaro's work has appeared in dozens of anthologies in England and the US. He is the author of three books for children: *Snail Stampede and Other Poems* (Hands Up Books), *Dancing With Frankenstein and Other Limericks* (Hands Up Books), and *Daddy Fixed the Vacuum Cleaner* (Willowisp Press). He lives in San Francisco with his wife, Diana, and his writing companion, a real cool dog named Addie.

Joshua Seigal is a poet, performer and educator who works with children of all ages and abilities. He has performed his poems at schools, libraries and festivals around the country, as well as leading workshops designed to inspire confidence and creativity. He has been described by teachers as 'inspirational' and 'a positive male role model'. www.joshuaseigal.co.uk

Kate Snow has been a newspaper journalist, a pop magazine writer and a book editor among other things. She writes poems for children with brain tumours for The Brain Tumour Charity. She is mum to Luke and Lily and her favourite things are writing poems for children (obviously), shopping, portrait painting, liquorice allsorts, shopping, dogs, brass bands (she plays euphonium in my local brass band) and shopping. Her website with an artist friend is www.snowflint.co.uk

Roger Stevens is a children's author and poet who visits schools, libraries and festivals performing and running workshops. He's written lots of poetry books and stories and runs the Poetry Zone, a website for children and teachers www.poetryzone.co.uk He lives in France and England (although not at the same time) with his wife and a very, very, very shy dog called Jasper.

Marian Swinger was born in Lowestoft, Suffolk, but now lives by the Thames in Essex with her partner, son, dog and chickens. For as long as she can remember, she has always loved to paint and draw and to write stories and poetry. She has been a professional photographer for most of her working life and has been writing poetry for children's anthologies for the past thirty years.

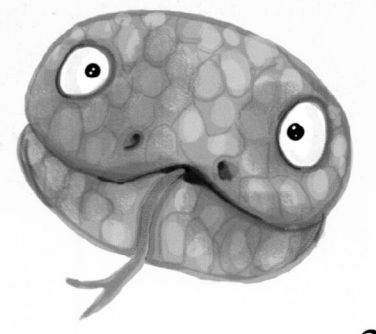

Index of first lines

Titles in the series:

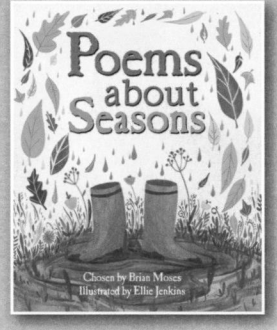